KID'S STORIES 2

ANOTHER COLLECTION OF GREAT MINECRAFT SHORT STORIES FOR CHILDREN

UNOFFICIAL MINECRAFT FICTION

BlockBoy

Table of Contents

The Cave

The tunnel

Kevin was surprised. He had not expected the cave to be empty. There wasn't a single cave spider to be seen. Kevin kept his bow ready, but as he looked around, he saw that it wasn't necessary.

The cave was empty. It was as simple as that.

Kevin was confused.

"The cave was empty. It was as simple as that."

Then what was the meaning of the message he had received?

Kevin's best friend Jared had sent him a message just hours before. It was short and urgent. All it said was – 'Come to the cave at these coordinates – 15N 63E 24L. Hurry up. It's very important!'

The moment Kevin had seen the message, he had rushed to the spot. He knew that Jared wouldn't leave a message like that unless there was something really exciting in the cave.

But Kevin didn't see anything. He was glad that there weren't any cave spiders around, but there weren't any treasure chests either. He had expected to find at least one inside the cave. But the cave itself was very small.

"Either Jared is playing a trick on me or something's wrong here," Kevin muttered to himself. As Kevin turned around to leave, something caught his eye. He noticed it quite by chance.

He saw a hollow space not far away.

"Wow, that looks like a tunnel," thought Kevin.

It was a tunnel. Kevin looked inside his inventory and pulled out a wooden stick and some flint. He took the torch and peered into the tunnel. He could sense that the tunnel looked deep and mysterious.

Where does it lead to?

He hesitated.

Then he thought about Jared. Kevin realized that Jared might have gone through the tunnel and was probably waiting for him at the other end.

Kevin grew excited.

"Maybe he's mining somewhere. Jared is always lucky," thought Kevin. "He might have found loads of diamonds somewhere."

Kevin walked faster through the tunnel. He was surprised that there were no mobs inside the tunnel either. Kevin walked for a very long time. The tunnel just seemed to go on and on.

Just as he was about to give up and walk away, Kevin saw a faint beam of light.

"Ah, at last... I think I've reached the other end," Kevin thought, sprinting across quickly.

He stepped out of the tunnel and took a deep breath. He looked all around. There was no sign of Jared.

"Jared," Kevin called out aloud. "Where are you?"

There was a loud rustle of leaves and Kevin turned around quickly.

Slenderman's evil scheme

It wasn't Jared. It was a tall, bony creature with a scarred face and wore a suit. Kevin froze on the spot. He hadn't expected to see Slenderman!

"It was a tall, bony creature with a scarred face and wore a long coat."

His bow was raised. Kevin quickly fixed an arrow and sent it whizzing straight at Slenderman. He dodged with such speed that Kevin was really surprised. He fixed another arrow and was about to shoot when he realized that Slenderman was gone. Kevin looked to the left and then to the right. He looked above and then turned around. Standing with a raised sword on his hand was Slenderman.

He winked at Kevin.

"Not quick enough, eh?" asked Slenderman. "Listen, kid. I'll spare you if you do what I say...

Kevin was already making a dash for the tunnel. He nearly made it, but what a shock! The tunnel was blocked.

Slenderman laughed aloud.

"There's no way out," he said. "Walk over here."

Kevin had no choice. Slenderman grabbed his bow, sword, arrows and armor.

"That's better," he muttered. Slenderman dragged Kevin to a building. He was pushed inside roughly. As the door slammed behind him, Kevin realized that there were many players inside.

He looked around in surprise. All the players were busy. Kevin suddenly noticed Jared. He was about to call out to him. But he realized that Jared wasn't even looking at him.

"Maybe he has a plan," Kevin thought. "I'll just pretend that I don't know anyone here."

"Teach him what to do. By the end of this week, everything should be ready. Otherwise I'll wipe you all out of Minecraft forever," Slenderman hissed fiercely.

SLAM!

The plan

He locked the door shut and left. There was silence for a long time. After what seemed to be a long time, Jared came rushing over to Kevin.

"Hey, Kevin," said Jared. "Sorry, old pal. I didn't mean to get you in trouble. I sent you a message when I spotted the tunnel. I didn't know that I'd get captured by Slenderman."

"That's okay," Kevin said. "But what's going on here?"

Other players crowded around Kevin and together they explained what was going on.

"Slenderman has terrible plans. He wants to destroy Minecraft little by little," said a player.

"He has set up TNT blocks in different places around here... in that island over there... in a village and other places," Jared said.

"What? That's horrible," Kevin gasped in horror.

"And we've all been captured to set off the TNT blocks," said Jared. "If we don't do it, Slenderman will torture us!"

"We don't want to do it..." cried the players. "Is there a way to escape?"

"The tunnel is blocked... but can't we build a portal to the Nether?" Kevin suggested.

"Do you have obsidian blocks with you? Jared asked.

"Yup, I have plenty of them. I mined them only yesterday" said Kevin. The others were really excited.

"But you have to be really careful when you build it," said a tall player. "Slenderman shouldn't find out..."

"But first, we'll have to find a way to diffuse all the TNT blocks," said Jared. The others agreed at once.

But, to do that somebody had to find out the main switch and turn it off.

Jared looked at Kevin. Kevin nodded.

"We'll do it," they told the other players.

Building the portal

They pretended to work while they looked out for Slenderman. When he entered the building, he looked around.

He checked everything.

"I want to make sure that nobody is cheating," said Slenderman. Then he went up the stairs and was gone for a long time.

When he came down he had an important announcement.

"Everything should be ready soon. We're blasting all our targets shortly," he said.

Kevin felt a chill creep down his spine.

After he left, Kevin and Jared crept upstairs. They had no weapon, and they were worried about what they'd find upstairs.

Guarding a room, were two Endermen. They had to think fast. It was this room that they had to enter, but how?

Jared whispered something. Quickly, Kevin hid while Jared boldly moved forward. The moment he made eye contact with the Endermen, they chased after him.

Kevin took the chance to open the room and went inside. He had to do the job quickly; otherwise Jared would get into big trouble with the Endermen. He didn't even have any weapon.

He looked around desperately. Finally, he noticed a small switch under a table.

"This must be it," thought Kevin. He looked around for any tool to disable it. And quite by luck, he spotted a pair of shears. Quickly, he cut off the redstone tripwire.

"Whew," sighed Kevin. The switch wouldn't work. He went out of the door and threw a bucket of water on one Enderman. Jared was already losing his health. Kevin dragged him along and ran down the stairs as he splashed water on the second Enderman.

It gave them the time to sprint down. They quickly built the Nether portal.

"They quickly built the Nether portal."

Jared whistled loudly, and the other players crowded around. They looked around and finally found a chest with all their weapons and armors.

One by one, they dropped through the portal.

Escape!

"Hurry up," Kevin cried out. Slenderman was back! And he'd gone upstairs.

A loud howl echoed everywhere. Slenderman had just discovered that the switch had been destroyed!

As he flew down the stairs, Jared and Kevin jumped through the portal. Kevin had a TNT block with him. Just as Slenderman rushed after them, Jared set off the TNT with flint and steel.

BOOM!

As the TNT exploded, the Nether portal was destroyed and Slenderman was captured inside!

"Hurray!" cried the players in delight. Slenderman was caught forever in his trap.

The players walked through the Nether world together. They had their weapons with them. Nobody was afraid. They felt victorious.

As for Slenderman, he was trapped forever. His plan to destroy Minecraft was ruined.

Sinister plot

The strange message

"But who could it be?" Simon asked.

The message did not include a name. All it said was:

"Meet me on the island in these coordinates. You are one of the special few selected. I promise you, you'll find something interesting here."

Simon was surprised. He and his friend Gamut had been invited. Simon wondered who else had received the invitation.

"Are you going?" Simon asked Gamut.

"We are going. What do we have to lose?" asked Gamut. "It sounds like this is going to be a very interesting trip."

Simon and Gamut landed on a bare island.

"Simon and Gamut landed on a bare island."

"What?" asked Simon, looking around. "Is this some kind of a joke?"

Gamut was surprised too. The island had nothing on it – no caves, no buildings, and absolutely no hiding place. There were just a few trees and a clump of bushes.

"We should never have fallen for it. It was probably some dumb trick," Simon complained.

But Gamut wasn't listening. He was looking at something in the distance.

"Does that look like a signboard to you?" Gamut asked, pointing to a tree in the distance.

"Gosh, yes..." said Simon. They hurried over to read what was written.

On the board was a short note.

"You're almost there. Make a boat and sail due south until you see an island with a tall white building."

"Good work, Gamut," Simon patted him on the shoulder. "Now let's build the boat. I've got some wood planks with me."

The island

Soon, they had a boat and headed south, looking out for an island. It was a long time and there were no islands in sight.

"Soon, they had a boat and headed south, looking out for an island."

"Maybe this is the real joke," Simon began again. They had been traveling in the sea for too long.

Gamut silently pointed ahead.

"Oh, it's here," said Simon, breaking into a grin. The island loomed closer and closer and the white building looked tall and formidable.

As Gamut and Simon stepped onto the island, they became aware that there were about ten other players.

One player looked at them and came over to greet.

"Welcome to my island. We've been waiting for you. I hope we have an interesting time together," he said, shaking their hands.

"Wow. So in the whole Minecraft world, it's only the twelve of us who has been invited?" Simon asked in surprise. He wasn't sure whether he felt flattered or worried.

"Yes. Now that we've all assembled, how about going into the building for a little chat?" asked the player. "Oh, call me Ben!"

The meeting

Ben led them into the building. They silently walked up a long flight of stairs and found themselves in a huge hall.

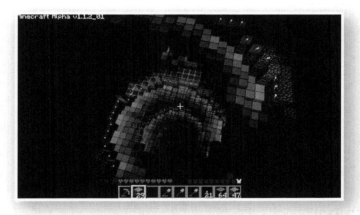

"They silently walked up a long flight of stairs and found themselves in a huge hall."

As they huddled together, Ben cleared his throat.

"I've invited you here to share something important. It is so special that nobody else in Minecraft should know about it," he said in a loud whisper.

Without waiting to hear what they had to say, Ben took a potion from the table and displayed it to everyone. It was sparkly purple in color and seemed to be alive. It was swishing and splashing around in the bottle.

"This is a very special potion and I made it quite by accident. I mean to make a potion of poison and ended up making this by adding a few other ingredients. Now what effect it has on mobs is interesting!" said Ben.

He flung a door open. Much to the players' shock, out came a skeleton. All the players hurried to pull out their swords and bows.

"Wait," said Ben with a grin. He threw the potion at the skeleton and almost immediately it slumped down on the ground. It swayed from side to side in a comical fashion.

"Hey, what is it doing? It isn't dead, is it?" one of the players asked. They were all fascinated by what was happening.

"No, but wait... there's more to come," said Ben. He went close to the skeleton and said, "Rise up and go attack Ruddy. Quick!"

Ruddy was shocked. The other players backed away in shock. The skeleton ignored everyone and headed straight towards Ruddy. But Ruddy was quick. He hid behind a pillar and shot arrows. The skeleton was quick too. It dodged, sprinted, ran and jumped around and came closer to Ruddy. Finally, it took him many blows from the sword to strike the skeleton down.

Ruddy was sweating all over.

"So what is this?" Gamut asked. He was dazed by what he saw.

The special potion

"Guys! This is my special potion of obedience. It works on mobs... and also on players!" said ben, looking proud. His eyes were gleaming.

The potion of obedience.

"Did you invite us just to show this?" Simon asked.

"No. I have a plan and I need you in my team. I have this brilliant idea to develop more potions with different ingredients. We can test it on each other and then use it on others. Everybody would have to listen to us and do what we bid! We'll have full control of the Minecraft world. We'll be the masters and everybody will be our slaves. Isn't that amazing?" Ben said. He was bubbling with excitement.

But he noticed that none of the players looked thrilled. He was disappointed.

"What's up? Don't you think this is awesome?" asked Ben.

Almost in unison, everybody shook their heads. It was fascinating but not in a good way.

"It's scary!" said Ruddy.

"It's wrong... I wouldn't want to control mobs or players," Josh said.

"It's not fair play. And it'll spoil the charm of the game," gamut pointed out. Simon nodded.

"Oh, I see..." said Ben. His tone was icy cold and bitter all of a sudden. "What a fool I am. I've picked all the wrong ones. I know hundreds who'd be happy to have a chance like this..."

"Good. Maybe you can send messages over to a new batch of players," said Simon, turning to leave. The other players were following him.

But Ben clapped twice.

Trapped

"Not so fast," he said. He activated a switch and suddenly the hall was closed from all sides. They were trapped inside.

"Think about my offer over the night. If you're not willing to accept, I'll be forced to use the obedience potion on everyone," he said, laughing loudly. "I'll probably make you all follow me like puppies..."

The players were furious. Gamut was thinking hard. A plan was forming inside his mind.

Then he called everyone together and told them what they could do. The others agreed that it was a good idea.

The next morning, they all lay around on the floor. Their swords and bows were scattered everywhere around them.

Ben came wheeling a huge cart full of potions. He wasn't going to take any chances with the players. But he noticed that the players were lying motionless.

"Hello," he called out.

Nobody stirred.

"HELLO! Wake up!" he shouted.

Still there was no movement. Ben got worried.

"Are you guys okay?" he asked, leaving his cart behind and knelt down beside Ruddy and Simon.

While Ben was busy, Gamut grabbed a potion and handed it over to a player. Slowly, the players passed the potions on, until everyone had one. They did it so silently that Ben didn't have a clue.

Attack time

Ben nearly fainted in shock, when the players slowly rose up like ghosts. When he saw the potions in their hands, he screamed and ran to his cart. It was empty. And it was too late to escape.

PLING!

CRASH!

THUNK!

SPLISH!

The potions rained on him from every direction. Ben crumpled on the ground and shivered.

"Listen to us," Gamut began. "You'll not make obedience potions anymore."

Then together they chorused, "You will not make any potions to enslave players or mobs. You will not ruin the Minecraft world in any way!"

Ben nodded.

"If you can open the door, we'll leave at once," said Ruddy.

Ben activated the switch at once. They rushed down the stairs and went outside. Gamut was gone for some time. Simon was waiting for him.

"Where did you go?" he asked.

"Oh, just one little thing. I destroyed his potion lab. I hope Ben will never remember to make any of his horrible potions again!" said Gamut.

"Perfect," said Ruddy.

The boats left quickly. The island grew smaller and smaller until the white building was nothing more than a speck.

"Wow, is anyone ever going to believe this?" asked Gamut. "That was one interesting afternoon!"

"Just concentrate on where we're headed," Simon said.

The Minecraft Club

The exclusive club

Everybody was talking about the club. The exclusive Minecraft Club – Mine Pros. Mine Pros had the cream of players. The best and most courageous players were part of the club.

The Minecraft club house.

They did exciting things! They organized trips through dangerous jungles and deserts. The club members went in search of Herobrine and hunted for Slenderman. They explored abandoned mineshafts, Nether fortresses and caves!

Jerry was just exploding with excitement. He imagined how glorious it would be to be a part of the club and do challenging things together. Jerry was a new player, he wasn't famous and he hadn't done anything outstanding yet. But he wanted to join the club.

"It's not easy, dude," his friend Gillian warned. "The players in the club are some of the oldest ones. They know tricks and things that we might have no clue about!"

"I'd still like to give it a shot," said Jerry.

Jerry had expected hesitation and even refusal to include him in the club. But what he'd not expected was scorn and mockery.

Lottie, the head of the club, laughed when Jerry told him that he wanted to join the club.

"Do you know what 'exclusive' means? It's only for the best of the best. We don't go around taking in everybody who is wandering around here."

"I might be new here, but I do like challenging tasks. How will you now I'm good until you test my skills?"

"Oh, look... he wants to prove his worth," one member hooted with laughter.

"Since he's begging to be included, maybe we should consider it..." said Dennis.

The challenge

"We'll give him a simple test. If he does the task, we'll see if he's worthy enough to be included," said Ryan.

"What do you say, kiddo?" asked Flynn.

Jerry just shrugged. He didn't like their tone or the way they laughed at him. But he wanted to join the club. He wanted to show them what he was capable of.

"Okay. Here's the deal. You'll go to this Wither Fortress in the nether world and deal with four Wither Skeletons there. Defeat all four, and we'll call you a champ!" said Ryan.

"Okay, where is it?" Jerry asked. After getting the coordinates from Ryan, Jerry stet off.

"Poor guy," said Dennis, shaking his head sadly. "Why did you send him off on such a dangerous mission? He doesn't even have a diamond sword with him."

"Who cares?" said Ryan. "I just wanted to get rid of him. He's never coming back!"

"Yea," said Lottie. "Nobody has returned alive after going on that mission!"

***

Jerry finished his Nether portal and activated with the flint and steel he had. As he ran into the Nether world, he didn't feel scared or upset. He didn't have any good weapons, but Jerry's specialty was not fighting. It was setting traps. He had always been interested in building traps and experimenting with them.

In the Nether world

When Jerry entered the Nether world, all his confidence seemed to see out. The lava waterfall and the bubbling pools did nothing to cheer him up. It was a dangerous world and one Jerry avoided if he could. He wished he was back in a nice jungle biome up in the Overworld.

"When Jerry entered the Nether world, all his confidence seemed to see out."

"What's the big deal?" Jerry muttered to himself. "Who cares if I don't get admitted in that club?"

But the next minute he knew he wanted to prove his worth. He didn't want those annoying fellows laughing and mocking at him. At this point his pride was at stake.

Jerry would have been killed if he hadn't looked up. But luckily he did! And there approaching him was one huge magma cube. Its fiery eyes gleamed and Jerry wasn't prepared to tackle it with his sword. He knew that it would be useless.

Jerry turned around and ran. With the magma cube hot in pursuit, he ran for his life. When he found a place to hide, he quickly pulled out his bow.

THWANG! WHIZZ!

Jerry heaved a sigh of relief as the arrows struck the target. Two more arrows later, the magma cube split into smaller cubes. This time, Jerry wasn't too worried.

He pulled out his sword and began to whack at them. There was only one left and as he tried to poke it, something else came in the way.

Zombie Pigmen!

Most unfortunately, Jerry struck a Zombie Pigman instead.

Provoked, the Pigman immediately began to chase after Jerry. Jerry noted that there were three more Pigmen chasing after him.

"Provoked, the Pigman immediately began to chase after Jerry."

Cursing his bad luck, Jerry made his way through the Netherrack, until he reached what looked like a cliff. He hesitated. He could try shooting arrows at them, but there was a better way. Jerry walked all the way to the edge of the cliff and weaved his way through the rocks until the Zombie Pigmen began following him.

They dashed blindly through the rocks and Jerry found the exact spot.

It was a dangerous curve that ended abruptly ended in a sheer drop. Jerry dashed ahead and then threw himself on a rock. But the Zombie Pigmen with no sense of direction, ran ahead and dropped all the way down.

Jerry stood up and ran as quickly as he could. He had to find the fortress quickly.

The Fortress

As Jerry walked towards the fortress, his heart beat rapidly. He knew that the mobs in the fortress were one of the toughest in Minecraft world.

There were the blazes, ghasts and the four Wither skeletons to deal with! Before setting out to the Nether world, Jerry had stopped at a snowy biome, emptied most of the unnecessary things in his inventory and packed a lot of snow. He'd learnt from his lessons that it was important to have some snow to deal with blazes. Each snowball inflicted enough damage to the blaze to deal with it easily.

The first mob he encountered in the fortress was a ghast. But Jerry was ready. He took out his iron sword and waved it menacingly at the ghast. He did not intend to kill the ghasts by striking with the sword.

Instead, Jerry waited for the ghast to shoot out fireballs.

THWACK!

ZHOOOP!

In one quick flash of movement, he deflected the fireball straight back to itself. The ghast was destroyed in no time.

Then there were a bunch of blazes darting around. Jerry hid himself behind a pillar and threw snowballs. He had a good aim and not a single snowball missed its target. In no time at all, the blazes were dealt with! Jerry had not lost his health fighting them with swords or arrows.

Before finding the Wither skeletons, Jerry had one more task. He began to build a platform near the corridor, several feet off the ground. He placed 22 blocks and looked satisfied. Now all he had to do was lure them to the platform.

Jerry slowly tiptoed around until he found the Wither Skeletons in a dark recess. The moment they saw Jerry, they came running towards him.

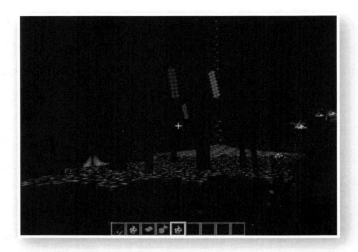

*"Jerry slowly tiptoed around until he found
the Wither Skeletons in a dark recess."*

The trap

The Wither Skeletons had arrows and Jerry
had a tough time, dodging them while trying
to find his way.

Jerry was ready.

He ran past the gap, across the corridor and
leapt straight onto the platform. He ducked

as the wither Skeletons came crashing down on the platform, one after another. But instead of halting to a stop, they went crashing all the way down.

Jerry heaved a sigh of relief. The fortress was empty. He had vanquished all the mobs inside.

But he knew that he should still look out for traps. A fortress that nobody had escaped alive would definitely have traps. Jerry crafted a redstone torch and carefully made his way. Sure enough, he noticed a pressure plate laid on the floor. If he'd not been looking for it, he would have definitely missed it. Then he noticed a treasure chest. He was about to walk to it when he noticed an unusual pattern of sand blocks around it.

"The falling sand trap," muttered Jerry, steering clear of it.

As he went back to report his success, he felt warm and powerful. He had defeated all the mobs in the fortress without using a sword or bow.

When the Mine Pros members heard about it, they were really surprised. Nobody they knew had managed to tackle the Wither Skeletons, all at the same time. Jerry's fame spread.

"That's totally awesome," they said. "Consider yourself a member already!"

"Hey, thanks," said Jerry. "But I've changed my mind. I'm going to start my own club!"

Spy club

Spying on Herobrine

"Are you sure?" Harry asked.

"I'm positive," said Jordan, looking through the binoculars. "Let's ask Ross. He's spying on them from the other end."

Jordan leapt down from the tree and Harry crawled out of the bush he'd been hiding in.

"This way," Jordan whispered and they crept low hiding behind trees and bushes and kept going until they reached a small hill.

Jordan whistled twice.

After some time, Ross came hurrying over to meet them.

"What did you see, Ross?" Harry asked.

"It's definitely Herobrine," Ross confirmed.

"You were right Jordan," said Harry. "Were you able to listen to what they were talking?"

"Only in bits... but I did hear that they were going to meet in the village down south, tomorrow," said Harry. "That's when they'll plan out where to attack next."

"Okay, let's get in touch with Jo and Ted. We need to have a meeting at once," said Harry.

Who is attacking the village?

Harry, Jordan, Ross, Ted and Jo were all members of the secret spy club in Minecraft.

There were many members across Minecraft with different identities. They mingled with the other players but kept their secrets to themselves. This particular group headed by Harry was investigating a particularly interesting case.

"The village"

For the past two weeks, there had been incidence of disturbances in different villages in a particular area. They had spent many hours looking around, talking to villagers and players and finally found out the information they were looking for.

"I'm sure it was Herobrine," said a player, who'd witnessed a building being destroyed. "I didn't seem him in close range, but I'll never forget those milky-white eyes!"

Another player said, "I didn't see Herobrine. But I did hear the sound of laughter. One friend of mine fell on the ground and was in a terrible state. He just kept repeating one name again and again..."

"Whose name?" Harry had asked.

"Slenderman," said the player. "He was there when the village was being attacked. I'm sure of it..."

Other players had seen nobody. A few villagers reported that they had seen players chopping up trees and destroying buildings.

It was getting more and more confusing.

"Are you sure?" Jordan asked.

"Yes. I saw it... We were so busy running away that I didn't take a better look. But they were definitely players," a priest villager said.

By a great stroke of luck, they found a farmer villager who'd actually seen Herobrine talking with a player. The message was, "Meet me near the cave!"

It was around this cave that Harry, Jordan and Ross had been spying. Ted and Jo were in a village looking out for anybody trying to create trouble.

Getting into action

"Jo, Ted... do you hear me?" Harry called out through the walkie-talkie. "Emergency meeting at our usual location. Please confirm."

Jo and Ted answered at once. "We'll be there shortly." The voice crackled and then there was only static.

In the tree house, Harry was waiting. Jordan and Ross were on either side, looking intently through their binoculars. They didn't want anybody anywhere close to their meeting place. As they looked around, they were satisfied.

Shortly, Ted and Jo came quietly, and hoisted themselves up the rope. Then the rope was lifted up and they went inside.

Harry spoke first, "We have reasons to believe that Herobrine meets up with a set of players and instructs them what damage to do. Sometimes, he asks them to chop down trees, other times they attack villages, mines and random players."

Ted said, "We have more news. A few players reported seeing Slenderman and Herobrine together in a forest."

"That's bad news. If they're teaming up, then they're probably planning to inflict some major damage. They are probably luring in players to join them," said Harry. "Their next meeting is in the village in the East. We need to be there and look for problems. We'll keep our eyes and ears open," said Harry.

The five members walked around the village, each going in a separate direction. They didn't want to attract attention by bunching up together and this way they'd be able to find out more. They had their walkie talkies with them. Whenever the coast was clear, they'd talk to each other to report something or get some information.

Harry was walking past a library, when he heard the walkie-talkie beep. He went into the library, found nobody inside and had a quick word.

"Herobrine is here. And it looks like he's sent a bunch of players to destroy a farm here," Ted reported.

Harry instructed everybody to gather at the spot where Ted was.

The vandals are caught

As they waited tensely, Jo spotted a player aiming his bow at an iron golem. Immediately, they positioned themselves behind different hiding spots and began to fire arrows at the player.

He was surprised when arrows started raining all around him. He couldn't see anyone around and surprised, he leapt off and sped away as fast as he could.

"Oh, I thought we'd be able to catch that guy," said Harry. It was frustrating. "At least we stopped him from destroying the iron golem. It'd have made it so much easier to destroy the farm so much easier for them. Now quick, let's hurry to the spot."

"Are you sure this is the one?" Harry asked Jo.

"Yes, Herobrine wanted the largest farm in the village destroyed. And this is the biggest one here," said Jo.

They positioned themselves at different corners and waited. Sure enough, a group of players jumped in through the fence and started whacking at the crops with their swords.

They had not expected anybody to be aware of it, and it made the job easy for Harry and his team. Ted, Harry and Jo had diamond swords held out while Ross and Jordan had a bow as well as potions.

When the players looked up, they were horrorstruck to see that they were surrounded.

Quickly, they tied them up with ropes and hauled them to an empty shed.

"Now spill the beans if you want to live," Harry said.

The evil plot

"We thought we'd do it for fun. I'm sorry. We won't do it again," said a player.

"Is this what Herobrine asked you to tell?" Jordan said. The players were shocked. They hadn't expected anybody to know their secret.

"Wait, don't do anything," said another player. "Herobrine and Slenderman wanted us to destroy villages and attack players. He wants to create havoc and chaos in the world so that they could slowly take control..."

"And what did they promise you?" asked Jo.

"They promised to give us parts of the world to control.

Harry laughed. "And were you stupid enough to believe that? They'd destroy you the moment their job was done! I'm sure they're using many other players for their dirty work."

"We'll leave them here. Let's meet Herobrine and Slenderman," said Harry.

***

"I hope the players didn't lie," said Jordan.

"No, I'm sure they're hiding here somewhere," Harry replied, trying to concentrate.

A loud rustle of leaves, made them turn around quickly.

"Hello kids. Looking for a job?" Herobrine asked. "Sorry. We're not hiring anymore."

Harry was furious. He sprinted forward and tried to thrust his sword straight at Herobrine. But before he could Slenderman leapt straight on top of him from a tree.

"He sprinted forward and tried to thrust his sword straight at Herobrine."

As Harry struggled to get free, Jo threw himself on Slenderman and whacked him on the head.

Jordan and Ted were trying to attack Herobrine, but he was so good at hiding.

Suddenly, both Herobrine and Slenderman vanished. They were looking around everywhere when suddenly they dropped from a tree again.

Driven away!

Ted's sword clattered to the ground and Jo's bow was pushed away. Herobrine attacked Harry and Slenderman had his hands gripped around Ross's neck.

"What a pity!" Herobrine said mockingly. "We'll have to put an end to these brave fellows."

But before he could do anything, he heard a low whistle. It was Harry. The next second a bunch of wolves surrounded Slenderman and Herobrine.

"The next second a bunch of wolves
surrounded Slenderman and Herobrine."

They were taken aback. They'd expected to deal with swords and arrows. That they could deal with. But wolves?

Slenderman tried to sneak behind a bush, but the wolf leapt straight in and dragged him out.

Herobrine found himself surrounded by the wolves.

They ran wildly as the wolves chased after them. Herobrine tried to whack them with his sword, but they leapt and caught his arm. Herobrine screamed as the wolf clamped his hand hard with its sharp teeth.

Slenderman had no better luck. The group heard the screams and howls of the two as they tried hard to escape from the wolves.

Next time they'd think twice before planning something like this," said Harry.

The Mineshaft Challenge

Time for action

The players looked at each other. It was easy to tell that they were all nervous yet excited. Who wouldn't be? They were participating in one of the toughest games in Minecraft – The Mineshaft Challenge. They were the only ones who'd made it to this level from the thousands of players who enrolled for the Mineshaft Challenge.

It wasn't easy. There were five players in total. The loudspeakers crackled to life.

"Hello everyone! Welcome to the biggest and toughest in Minecraft – The Mineshaft Challenge. It's no easy task. The competitors will go through hardships and dangers in an abandoned mineshaft and face mobs and look out for traps. The five players may enter into the mineshaft through separate entrances. There are no tools or weapons allowed. They can be found hidden in there, but until then, the players will use their brains and powers to survive there. Even food is packed away in different treasure chests. Find them and you'll make it, otherwise hunger will get the better of you!

And that's not all. The player who first finds the Mineshaft Trophy and makes it to the exit first is the winner. Finders aren't always the keepers, as the players will find out.

Ready? Off you go!

Where's the entrance?

The players dashed madly from their start positions. And since it was not any ordinary game, even finding the entrance to the mineshaft was not straightforward. Jamie, Harley, Danny, Tex and Archie looked around desperately trying to find the entrance.

Quite by luck, Tex fell through a hole and slid all the way down and dropped straight into the mineshaft. After a long time, Archie found a small tunnel in a cave and went through it and found the mineshaft opening.

"After a long time, Archie found a small tunnel in a cave and went through it and found the mineshaft opening."

Jamie slipped on a rock and went sprawling on the ground. That was quite a good thing because he found the entrance hidden behind a bush. Harley cursed his luck as he spotted an Enderman. He ran away as fast as he could and that turned out to be a good thing because he soon found a way in. Harley walked around everywhere and was almost about to give up when he finally spotted the entrance. Sighing, he entered. His health bar wasn't full even before entering the mineshaft.

But Harley was lucky enough to stumble upon a treasure chest within a few seconds. He opened it eagerly, hoping that there would be a sword inside, but all it had was food. But it was still a lucky find and Harley gladly threw it into his empty inventory.

Tex had not been so lucky. He'd dropped on the hard floor and had almost immediately been surrounded by some spiders almost immediately. He scrambled as quickly as he could manage and tried to find higher ground to stand on. He found a torch on the wall and gladly took it. The flickering light was a source of comfort in the darkness.

Inside the mineshaft

He pointed the torch at the spiders and they backed away. Slowly, looking everywhere around, Tex made his way inside. Jamie found the wall and slowly traced his steps, along the wall hoping to find a chest. He didn't want to face a mob unarmed, and the sooner he found something useful, the better!

"He pointed the torch at the spiders and they backed away."

Danny had an interesting time, running away first from spiders, and then from a skeleton that chased after him. Thankfully, it had only a sword and not a bow, so he ran fast as he could. He dashed ahead blindly and he forgot all about the traps.

As he set foot on a pressure plate, he went plunging all the way down! Not far away, Archie had managed to walk a few steps when he saw a platform and spiders! He stood on the platform and aimed blows on it with his hand.

BIFF! THUD!

But the spider followed him as he stumbled ahead. And at that moment, Archie noticed a pressure plate. He carefully weaved his way past it and position himself behind it. When the spider jumped, he sprinted away quickly.

It landed on the plate and the TNT went off at once.

BOOM!

There were more spiders all over the place and skeletons walked around. Archie weaved along, creeping away from them.

Treasures and Dangers

The players found different treasure chests as they made their way through the mineshaft. Usually mineshafts had about four exit points. But because the Mineshaft Challenge was a tough game, all exits except one had been blocked.

Harley had made his way to two exits and had returned in agony because it had been blocked. He had to check out the other two exits, mark the right one and then hunt for the trophy. He had found some lapis lazuli in one of the treasure chests and he had some wool with him. He decided to use the blue-dyed wool as a marker.

Both Danny and Tex had been lucky enough to find some shears in their treasure chests. With all the cobwebs hanging everywhere around the place, it made the job of hacking at them easier.

As Jamie slashed at more cobwebs with his sword, he was worried that it was going to dull it soon.

Danny was amazed by the amount of treasure chests scattered along the way. He wondered why the toughest game in Minecraft had so many treasures.

He got the answer almost immediately. The place had just about as many dangers to compensate for the treasures.

He saw a bunch of mobs travelling around in mine carts and made a run for it. The zombies and skeletons jumped out of the carts and started running after Danny. He tried his best to avoid the arrows, but it was getting really difficult.

The other players had also encountered these mobs. It seemed almost as if the entire mineshaft was laid with powered rails with mob-packed mine carts speeding around everywhere.

They ran, hid, stumbled, fell and made their way past the mobs.

More perils

Archie found some melon seeds and bread in a chest and took them gratefully. He was already low on his health, and he was glad about the find.

BANG!

Archie had banged his head against yet another treasure chest. He though that it was his lucky day.

 "Yes," Archie pumped his fist as he found a sword. He felt much safer with it.

Jamie tried to make it to a dark shape in the corner. It looked like a chest and he hoped that it would be food because his health bar was almost completely drained. He crawled slowly, but he had not an ounce of strength left. Before he could open it, he fell down on the ground.

Tex was so busy backing away while scaring off some spiders with the torch that he didn't notice the lava pool behind him. As his foot slipped, he tried to find something to hold on. But he found nothing, and went hurling into the pool!

When Archie found a pedestal with the trophy on it, he could hardly believe his eyes. Tucking hiss sword under his shirt, he pulled the trophy and started running. He had to find the exit. The next minute, somebody grabbed the trophy from him.

Harley sprinted and hopped, making his way to the exit. He'd already found out where it was. Archie followed him, trying to get the trophy back. And quite by accident, Harley tripped and went sprawling on the floor.

Archie pulled out his sword and struck him twice.

With Harley taken care of, all Archie had to do was find the exit. And as Archie dashed blindly right ahead, he passed one mob after another. It was almost as if they had all decided to swarm the place around the exit.

Archie was getting weaker and weaker, as he slashed at zombies, skeletons and spider jockeys.

The trophy

In the distance he heard the sound of footsteps. Harley wasn't far behind. Archie clutched the trophy with all his might and hastened. He kept looking backward and ran on and on.

All of a sudden he was running on a narrow platform. It took him some time to realize where he was and he slowed down just in time. He held on to the wall as he inched forward, too scared to look down.

But Harley hadn't been lucky. He was inches away from Archie and had almost grabbed the trophy. But he'd missed the platform completely and went plunging down into the lava pool.

Along that narrow passage, a skeleton came running. Just as it took its bow, Archie reacted with lightning speed with the last ounce of strength.

THWANG!

The blow was so powerful that it sent the skeleton tethering to the edge.

PLOP!

That was the end of the skeleton. Archie dragged himself to the end of the platform. He was too weak to move anymore. He dropped down heavily on a chest. Slowly he managed to get it open.

When he saw what was inside, he smiled weakly. Then he ate the golden apple and stood up. He held the trophy above his head and marched straight ahead.

When he ran out of the exit, a big crowd cheered him.

"Congratulations!" the announcer called out. "You've won the Mineshaft Challenge. You've also entitled yourself to a trip to Island 424 for the next big challenge – The Island survival! You know the rules – you start off with an empty inventory and survive on what is found on the island. Are you up for the challenge?"

The crowd cheered. Archie was ready.

Slime invasion

Slimes everywhere

When Fred came back to his castle after a long mining expedition, he was devastated to see that it was infested with slimes.

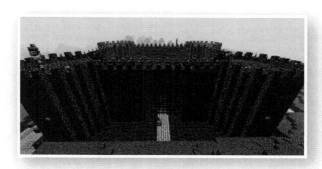

Fred's castle

Slimes were no big deal. He'd encountered many slimes in Minecraft. They were much easier than Skeletons or Endermen. But there were too many slimes to tackle. When he'd opened the door he'd got the shock of his life.

Slimes were just about everywhere like some kind of a spreading mold.

Fred knew that arrows were useless. He'd whacked ta a few with his sword, but there was a monster spawner somewhere inside.

If it had been just another building, Fred wouldn't have cared. But it was his castle – a castle he'd built over several weeks. He had no intention of letting a bunch of slimes get away with occupying his castle.

"I'll find a way to get rid of them," Fred muttered to himself. The first person who came to his mind was Eric.

Eric had once been stuck in a swamp area and had to deal with many slimes. Fred didn't remember what his strategy was, but he still thought it was much easier to deal with them out in the open than inside a castle – his castle!

Finding Eric

Fred found Eric where he usually hung around – in the village closest to his castle. Eric was chatting with a blacksmith when Fred approached him.

"Hey, man... what's up? Trading here?" Eric asked.

Fred shook his head.

"Eric, it's important," Fred said, lowering his voice. "My castle is chock full of slimes. And I need help clearing them out. Since you're the expert when it comes to slimes, I thought I'd ask you for help."

Eric looked serious.

"These slimes..." Eric began. "Are they different? Did you notice something strange?"

"I don't know," Fred confessed. "I didn't look properly. I just took a few swipes at slimes close to the door. But when I saw how hopeless it all was, I just gave up and came over to find you."

"Good," said Eric grimly. "In fact, I have a feeling that these are no ordinary slimes. Neither were the ones that I encountered in the swamp."

"What do you mean?" asked Fred.

"Slimes just don't come, spawn and take over a player's castle... There's more to this than we know," said Eric. "Come let's go there at once!"

Before long, Eric and Fred were circling the castle, looking through windows. There was no doubt that the place was just oozing with slimes. Eric stared at them for a long time and then beckoned Fred.

"They're not ordinary slimes. Just look at them for a while," said Eric.

Creeping inside...

Fred looked through the window. Eric was right. Something wasn't right about the slimes. They weren't just hopping about randomly. They hopped along for some time, and then a group of slimes stood together in a cluster and seemed to have some kind of a meeting. Then they resumed hopping and once again gathered together.

The slimes

It looked so strange. It was almost as if they'd been altered in some way. Yes, that was it!

"Eric, do you think they are mutants of some sort?" Fred whispered.

"Most possibly..." Eric nodded. "First we have to find out a way to enter your castle and attack them."

Fred pointed out to ivy growing on one side. Silently, they hoisted themselves up the ivy and reached as close they could manage to an open window on the top.

Eric peered in.

"The coast is clear," he whispered and jumped into the empty room.

"I wonder why this room hadn't been occupied by the slimes. Maybe they haven't made it to the top floor yet," said Fred, heaving a sigh of relief.

"Let's hope so," said Eric. Very cautiously, they opened the door and looked out. It was still empty in the corridor.

As they rounded the corner, they heard the sound of footsteps and retreated to a dark recess where they hoped they wouldn't be visible. Two zombies were walking by, whispering to each other.

The zombies' conversation

"Now that we've bitten these slimes, all we have to do is wait. We'll make that secret potion and make them do everything we want," said one zombie.

"I wish there was a way to make them invincible. That way, we won't have to worry about them getting destroyed. They'll take over Minecraft and it'll be all ours," said the other zombie.

"Our boss should be happy with the results. He wants us to come over to his lab later today, so that we can bite some spiders. He thinks zombiefied spiders can be more dangerous," said the first zombie.

Eric and Fred shivered uncontrollably. It sounded terrifying. He wondered who the 'boss' was and what other plans he had to take over Minecraft. Until they destroyed the slimes, there really wasn't much hope.

"Let's first look around. You've got your sword?" asked Eric. They soon found out that the slimes had occupied most of the bottom space and were slowly filling up space everywhere.

"Maybe, once the castle is full, it bursts open and releases them everywhere around?" Fred suggested.

Acting Quickly

But before Eric could answer, they heard a moan. The zombies had spotted them. There was nothing to do but attack. Eric and Fred caught the zombies completely by surprise. They'd not expected to see anyone inside. They tried to attack the zombies but they dodged very efficiently.

Seeing no other option, Eric and Fred ran. The zombies were hot in pursuit but Eric and Fred had an advantage because Fred knew his castle well and before long, they'd made it to the other side and the zombies were nowhere in sight. They knew that any minute the zombies would alert the slimes and they would all come in search of them.

Quickly, they got into a room and set into action at once. They dug a deep pit and filled it with buckets of lava. Then they placed a TNT block about 3 blocks down and fixed a pressure plate over it. They repeated it until there were pressure plates around the pit. After lining the whole set up with gravel, they waited tensely.

Then close to it, they designed more traps on all sides and filled them with water. Then they waited and listened. There was a loud buzz of activity downstairs. The zombies had probably warned the slimes and they were all hopping upstairs like mad creatures. Eric ran forward and stood in front of them so that they wouldn't miss him and then ran back through the door.

"They're coming," he cried out and together they hid in a corner.

The End... or is it?

The zombies were the first to arrive. They crashed open the door and looked around. Without thinking, they stepped forward and stepped right onto the pressure plates. They realized almost immediately that it was a trap but it was too late.

CRASH! FIZZZ!

They fell into the lava pit and splashed around helplessly. Soon it became silent.

But the slimes were already arriving. They swarmed around the place and a few fell into the pit, but the others had managed to steer clear of the lava pit. But they did not escape the other pits dug everywhere.

PLOP! PLOP!

They fell, one by one, into the pits full of water. Eric and Fred waited. They had all the time in the world. They thought the slimes would never stop falling into the pits, but eventually it grew silent again.

All that remained were a handful of slimes. They attacked them with their swords and afterwards they dealt the tiny slimes with their hands.

When they explored the whole castle and found that there were no more slimes left, Eric and Fred heaved big sighs of relief.

"But it's hardly over," Eric reminded him. "There are more slimes around Minecraft and we have no idea who the boss is…"

"Maybe we should set off to find out what this is," Fred suggested.

Village Troubles

Horrid pranks

"Aww, not again" Harry complained.

"What happened this time?" asked Uber.

Harry was a librarian villager. And nothing was more annoying than books scattered all over the floor. This had been going on for some time. Harry wondered who'd do things like that.

Harry

"Surely it's not some mob? Maybe an Enderman or a Witch..." Harry wondered, but Uber shook his head.

"Mobs don't do things like this. At least normally they don't..." said Uber. "There's something going on in the village. Let's check with Smith and Rex!"

As they walked towards Rex's butcher shop, they saw Smith there too. From the way they were talking agitatedly, Uber and Harry realized that things had gone wrong.

"Rex, what happened?" Harry called out.

"Stolen! My cooked chicken and pork chops are all gone. I can't let someone steal my stuff every day. My business will be ruined completely," Rex said.

Smith was angry too. Somebody had destroyed all the items in his shop. He'd worked hard all week to make chainmail chest plates, boots and helmets. But they were all hacked with a sword so badly that it was unusable. All his hard work had been wasted.

Silas's glow stones and redstone dust were missing. He'd thought it would be safe locked up, but the wardrobe had been broken open. Farmer Brown's house had been raided and his stock of cookies, bread, apples, pumpkin pies and cake were missing.

Getting the spy team ready

Everybody was looking really gloomy.

"There is only one way to set things right. We'll have to get together for a meeting," said Uber.

The message was sent across and villagers from all corners of the village gathered together outside the library.

Since most of their items had been stolen or destroyed, the villagers didn't have anything much to trade so they decided that they might as well go to the meeting. They were also very anxious to find out a way to stop the problem. If it went on this way, they'd be ruined.

Uber cleared his throat.

"Fellows, we all know what has been happening in our village in the past few days. Things are stolen, food is taken and items are destroyed. Why would anyone do this to us? We'll have to find out. I have a suggestion..."

"Tell us," the villagers chorused.

"I want four or five volunteers to help me spy on the village. I'll also talk things with the iron golem. Together, we should be able to find out who it is," said Uber.

The villagers thought it was a good plan. Harry, Will, Ken, Moll and Uber set off at once. They decided to walk through the village in different directions and meet up again at the library.

"Remember, if you see something strange or find somebody suspicious, just send a message to me quickly," Uber instructed.

But he villagers did not find anything odd. There were just a few players trading with the villagers. There were no mobs anywhere around.

Uber went to see the iron golem and told him to be ready whenever they called him. The golem promised solemnly.

The iron golemn

For four days, they looked everywhere and kept their eyes and ears open. At the end of the day, they talked about what they found.

In the evening, they met outside the library.

"Any luck?" Uber asked.

The others shook their heads. Uber told them that he hadn't spotted anything strange either.

"Come, let's just talk about what we saw. We might get some clues," said Uber. "We'll go into the library, so that nobody will hear us."

Pranksters captured

So Uber and the other villagers met up inside the library. It was dark inside but the villagers did not mind. They were talking in very low voices when suddenly they heard a sound.

First they thought it was Harry. But it sounded like a lot of books had crashed to the floor.

"Wait," said Uber suddenly. "Harry has gone to visit Rex... somebody else is inside..."

Uber looked around and spotted a player toppling more books in the corner.

"Hey, you…" Uber called out at once.

The player was shocked. He hadn't expected anyone to be around.

"You can't catch me, you stupid villagers," the player called out cheekily, as he ran out.

Outside, he whistled loudly.

"Guys, come on, let's leave…" he said. "I've been spotted."

In the dark, Uber and the other villagers made out about five players running.

"Don't come near us," one player warned. "I won't hesitate to use my sword on you!"

Uber didn't bother to run after the players. He whistled loudly tree times.

THUMP! THUMP!

And all of a sudden, the iron golem stood directly in front of the players. That was another rude shock for them. They hadn't expected the golem to be anywhere around. The iron golem usually roamed around the edge of the village.

The players had swords, but the golem was stronger and more powerful. As the players tried to fight it with swords, the golem dealt a few fierce blows sending them flying to the ground. The players quickly realized that they were no match to it. Their swords had gone and they were helpless. To make it worse, Uber and the others were standing all around them. They quickly tied up the players and dragged them into the nearest building.

"Let us go..." they begged. "We were just playing some pranks. We didn't really harm anyone."

"Well, we aren't harming you either," Uber told them. "A few days locked up inside this building will teach you not to play the fool here."

All the villagers came to see the pranksters. The players felt terrible. They knew that they had gone too far. But they had no choice but to remain imprisoned inside, until they were released.

Zombie Villager Invasion

The next day, Uber was standing alone when he heard voices. He had done so much spying in the last week, that his senses had grown sharp.

The voices sounded very strange. He crept slowly until he came across some thick bushes. As he peered out of the bush, he was horrified to see that there were about a bunch of zombie villagers.

"As he peered out of the bush, he was horrified to see that there were about a bunch of zombie villagers."

When he listened to their plan, he went pale. Without wasting any time, he rushed back and gathered everyone together.

"I just heard something terrible. A band of zombie villagers are planning to attack us. We need to do something quickly. I'm going to alert the iron golem," said Uber.

"How are we ever going to get away?" the villagers asked. Everybody was scared.

Unexpected help

Harry was speaking to Uber about different ways to tackle the zombies.

"Uber, wait… one iron golem isn't going to be enough to tackle them…" Harry was saying.

They were holding the discussion in the same building where the players were held as prisoners.

And they heard everything that they were talking.

They rapped against the bars of the prison. Harry and Uber looked up, irritated. They were annoying enough playing pranks. But now that they were in a prison, they still seemed to be intent on annoying them.

"What do you want?" Harry asked. "We're discussing something very important and confidential!"

"Confidential?" The players laughed. "We could hear every word of it!"

Uber groaned and Harry shook his head.

"Listen... we're willing to help you," one player said. "If you could only release us..."

Harry and Uber looked at them in surprise.

"We not only promise to help you tackle the zombies, but we'll also never play any pranks. Please?"

The players sounded sincere.

Uber and Harry had a whispered conversation.

Uber gulped. "Do you think they would?"

"Yes, if we promise to release them..." said Harry.

It turned out that the players were willing to help them out.

The attack on the zombies

"We're doing this not just to get released, but also as a favor. We're truly sorry," said one of the players.

The players had a hurried meeting with the other villagers. They told them about a plan they had. The players would hide in trees and keep their bows ready. The villagers could lead the zombie villagers directly to that place.

"I think this would work," Uber said excitedly.

So when the zombie villagers slowly spread across the village, everybody was ready. The villagers ran and led the zombies straight to the place where the players were waiting.

The moment they did that, the players began to shoot arrows at remarkable speed.

The zombie villagers couldn't understand what was happening. The villagers ran to hide while the zombies fell down on the ground.

The iron golem also attacked the zombie villagers.

BIFF!

THUD!

CRASH!

OOWWWWW!

Before long, they were all vanquished. There was rotten flesh scattered everywhere. The villagers sighed in relief.

"You were terrible pranksters... but you did help us out in time of need. We shall be friends," said Uber.

The players shook hands with everyone before leaving. They promised to pay a visit as soon as they could. "But no more pranks anymore," they assured, before leaving.

The Coven

The Problems

The players soon realized that there was a big problem. It wasn't easy going about with their normal work there. Nobody could mine in peace, because sooner or later they were attacked by cave spiders.

But all mines have cave spiders and while it is a little tricky to deal with them, it's not really difficult. But the cave spiders they found around that region were monstrous to start with. They were also super-fast and attacked more ferociously than the usual ones. It wasn't easy to escape from them.

And that was not the only problem. The villages near the mine got attacked way too often. If it wasn't zombies, it was skeletons. The villagers had long forgotten to trade, as they were busy running away from one danger after another.

The trees exploded all of a sudden. Strange mushrooms grew in patches and any player who was silly enough to eat them suffered terrible hallucinations and agony. And with no warning, a player would suddenly zip past at lightning speed, knocking away everyone else in the path.

First, nobody had a clue what was happening. They just thought that something strange was happening in that place. It would have been easy to avoid the place altogether. But the place was full of mines. The players knew that it was packed full of diamonds, coal and lots of useful things.

The witches

After a while, a player spotted a witch. Then more players spotted witches hanging around in different spots. First they thought that witches were the common mobs in that area.

"After a while, a player spotted a witch."

And they were tough to tackle when they were together. They hurled potions at the players at the same time, making them several folds slower and unable to attack quickly enough. It was hopeless to try and attack the witches when they stood together. They were a bunch of formidable mobs.

It also became clear that all the strange things happening around the place was due to these witches. They prepared special potions for the spiders to make them faster and fiercer. They threw potions at zombies and skeletons to make them twice as dangerous. They made trees explode and grew mushrooms for their enchantments.

Nick had heard a lot about the witches plaguing the area around the mines. He wasn't called 'Slick Nick' without a reason. He was quick, clever and smart and that helped him survive in the toughest biomes in Minecraft. In fact, he took it as a challenge to try and survive in abandoned mineshafts, zombie-infested villages or deserts.

When he'd heard that more and more players were giving up their quest to explore the mines, Slick Nick was very interested.

He went there at once. The first thing that Nick did was to build a castle right in the middle of the mines. His first intention was of course to have a safe place to stay in, so that he could look around and catch the witches causing all the trouble. But more important than that was that he wanted to build traps. Nick was crazy about traps and he'd been interested in them more than anything else. He was an expert in different types of traps.

From Nick's experience, fighting with swords wasted a lot of energy and health. He'd found traps more efficient if only there was a way to lure the players and mobs inside the castle.

Nick was confident that the witches would definitely visit the castle. They'd be curious to find out who was daring enough to build a castle right in the middle of the place they terrorized.

But first, Nick decided to spy around the place and find out where the witches met. That would be very useful to destroy them.

Spying around

Nick took a bow and some arrows as well as his sword as he set off. While Nick specialized in traps, he was also really good at fighting. He wasn't afraid of the witches – he'd seem worse mobs in his life in Minecraft.

Nick went around carefully. First, he climbed up a tree and looked around for a long time. Then he made his way slowly, climbing trees often to make sure that the place was free from mobs. Finally he reached a clearing. There were more wild mushrooms there than anywhere else.

Nick couldn't help thinking that the witches might be there. He didn't wait for a second. He hoisted himself u p a tree and that too just in time. A group of witches arrived there and looked around. They had no idea that Nick was spying on them from atop the tree.

"Did you see that castle out there?" one witch asked.

"I sure did. That's not a good sign. We don't want anyone around..." said another witch.

"And these bold players only spell trouble," said a third witch.

"Don't worry," said the first witch. "Nobody is going to find our hiding place. As long as nobody does that, we're as good as safe!"

"How about paying a visit there tonight?" asked another witch.

"That we'll do," the witches agreed.

Nick watched the witches slowly disappear behind a bush. After some time, Nick dropped down from the tree and pushed aside the bush. As he'd guessed, there was a tunnel leading somewhere.

It was so well-hidden that unless someone had sat on the exact same tree and watched the witches disappear, it would have been impossible to find out.

Nick wondered if it would be a good idea to go inside the tunnel. But then he thought that it wasn't the smartest thing to do. He would be pitted against a bunch of witches and an easy target for them.

He decided to wait for them to pay a visit. And they did that very evening.

In Nick's castle

Nick's castle.

Nick was ready. The moment he spotted them, he sneaked out. He knew that there was no better time to go into that tunnel. His castle was full of traps and he hoped that the witches would have a good time there.

The first witch to enter the castle turned right and went straight through the stairs, keeping the splash potion ready. Another witch followed close behind. Two other witches went on to explore the other part of the house.

AAAAAHHH!

The two witches walking downstairs leapt up in surprise when they heard the sound.

As they hurried up, they saw what had happened. One of the witches had stepped on a platform and went hurling several blocks down.

Another witch was walking along when she spotted a door on the left. She wondered if Nick was hiding somewhere inside. With a potion ready in her hand, she opened it.

She did not notice the button at the entrance. As she stepped on it, the pressure plate underneath got activated.

BOOM!

The TNT hidden in the pits beyond the door blew up the unfortunate witch.

She was another victim of the exploding door trap that was Nick's favorite. He'd trapped many players and mobs using it.

Not knowing what had happened, the other witches went around looking for Nick.

One witch found a curious little block with a sign 'Do not disturb. Busy mining!'

The witch cackled. "I'm coming right away," she said and stepped onto the block. She stepped on the sign and broke it.

WHOOSH!

The witch fell down a long way. It was a greedy man's grave! This time it was not diamonds or loot the victim was after – it was Nick.

The witch fell so far down that nobody even heard her screams and none of her potions could help her stop the long, long fall!

All Gone!

But tow witches managed to remain uncaught. They hunted for the others and grew alarmed. They were nowhere to be seen!

"This isn't good," one witch said in a shaky voice. "Let's move out at once. This place gives me the creeps!"

They managed to get out of the house alive. They rushed immediately to the tunnel.

When they went inside, it was empty. They had no idea that Nick had paid a visit inside and was hiding outside eagerly waiting to see what would happen.

Nick had used redstone dust, redstone torches, glass, cobblestone, lava, repeaters and a trapped chest. He hoped that the witches would get curious enough to open the chest.

Sure enough, that was the first thing they saw.

"Hey, this wasn't here before," said one witch. They went over to open it.

"Wait, it could be a trick," the other witch screamed, but it was too late. The moment the chest was flung open, the pistons underneath were activated, and the floor gave away. The witches screamed as they fell into the lava pool underground.

Nick smiled when he heard their screams. The job was done. He'd saved the place from a nasty bunch of witches without lifting the sword once!

MORE MINECRAFT BOOKS YOU SHOULD CHECK OUT:

Minecraft: Genesis - A Legend of How It All Began: A Minecraft Novel ft. Herobrine, Notch, Junkboy and Jeb

Minecraft Comic Book Collection: A Series of AWESOME Minecraft Comics

Minecraft: Ultimate Book of Secrets & Mysteries: 30 AWESOME Secrets You Never Knew About REVEALED

13109074R00068

Printed in Great Britain
by Amazon.co.uk, Ltd.,
Marston Gate.